Dear Parent:
Your child's love of reading starts here!

Every child learns to read in a different way and at his or her own speed. Some go back and forth between reading levels and read favorite books again and again. Others read through each level in order. You can help your young reader improve and become more confident by encouraging his or her own interests and abilities. From books your child reads with you to the first books he or she reads alone, there are I Can Read Books for every stage of reading:

SHARED READING
Basic language, word repetition, and whimsical illustrations, ideal for sharing with your emergent reader

BEGINNING READING
Short sentences, familiar words, and simple concepts for children eager to read on their own

READING WITH HELP
Engaging stories, longer sentences, and language play for developing readers

READING ALONE
Complex plots, challenging vocabulary, and high-interest topics for the independent reader

ADVANCED READING
Short paragraphs, chapters, and exciting themes for the perfect bridge to chapter books

I Can Read Books have introduced children to the joy of reading since 1957. Featuring award-winning authors and illustrators and a fabulous cast of beloved characters, I Can Read Books set the standard for beginning readers.

A lifetime of discovery begins with the magical words "I Can Read!"

Visit www.icanread.com for information
on enriching your child's reading experience.

I Can Read Book® is a trademark of HarperCollins Publishers.

Guinness World Records: Daring Dogs
Copyright © 2016 Guinness World Records Limited.
Guinness World Records and related logos are trademarks of Guinness World Records Limited.
All records and information accurate as of February 1, 2015
www.icanread.com

Library of Congress Control Number: 2014959384
ISBN 978-0-06-234183-9 (trade bdg.)—ISBN 978-0-06-234182-2 (pbk.)
Typography by Victor Joesph Ochoa

16 17 18 19   PC/WOR   10 9 8 7 6 5 4 3   ❖   First Edition

I Can Read!

READING 2 WITH HELP

GUINNESS WORLD RECORDS

DARING DOGS

by Cari Meister

Photos supplied by
Guinness World Records

HARPER
An Imprint of HarperCollinsPublishers

Augie, a golden retriever, kept the **most tennis balls in his mouth at one time**—5. His amazing trick has earned him lots of dog treats!

Monkey kept a level head

to **balance the most biscuits**

on her nose at once—26!

Anastasia burst 100 balloons with her teeth in 44.49 seconds. She set the doggy record for the **fastest time to pop 100 balloons**.

Tubby is one eco-friendly hound! He set the record for **most bottles recycled by a dog**. He gathered about 26,000 bottles on his walks over 6 years.

Tigger holds the all-time
world record for the **longest ears**.
His right ear was 13.75 inches long.
His left ear was a little smaller
at 13.5 inches long.

Harbor, a coonhound from Colorado, has the **longest ears of any living dog**. His right ear measures 13.5 inches. His left ear is 12.25 inches long.

These guys must eat a lot!

They are Old English Mastiffs.

Male mastiffs weigh between

170 and 200 pounds.

They share the record for **heaviest dog breed** with the St. Bernard.

Great Dane Morgan (right) was the **tallest female dog**.

She was 3 feet, 2.6 inches tall.

Zeus was the **tallest dog ever**.

Also a Great Dane,

he was 3 feet, 7 inches tall.

Chihuahua Cupcake

is the **smallest service dog**.

She visits patients in the hospital

to brighten their days.

She is only 6.25 inches tall

and 14.25 inches long.

Greyhound Cinderella May
cleared a jump of 68 inches,
setting the record for the **highest
jump by a dog**.
That's about the height
of a refrigerator!

Jack the Black, a rescue dog, set a world record in 2013 during a training exercise. The Newfoundland **pulled a person 25 meters from water to the shore** in 1 minute and 36 seconds!

Border collie–Kelpie cross
Ozzy set the record
for **fastest tightrope crossing**
in 2013.
He cleared the 11-foot, 5.7-inch
stretch in 18.22 seconds!

Jiff, a Pomeranian,
set *two* world records.

For **fastest 10 meters on hind legs**,
Jiff traveled about 33 feet
in 6.5 seconds on his back legs.

For **fastest 5 meters on front legs**,
Jiff went about 16 feet
in 7.76 seconds on his front paws.

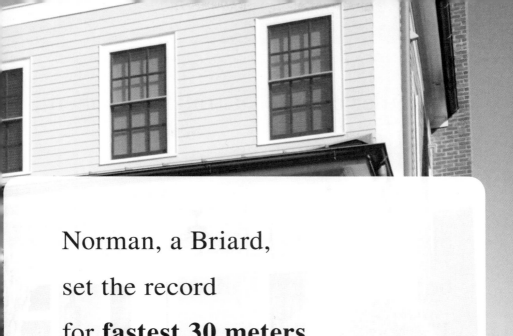

Norman, a Briard,
set the record
for **fastest 30 meters
on a scooter**.
He rode just under
100 feet in 20.77 seconds.
Norman rides with his
front paws on the handlebars.
He uses one hind leg to balance
and the other hind leg to push.

A border collie–Australian shepherd, Sweet Pea can boast three world records. She **walked *up* 17 steps balancing a glass of water**. Then she **walked *down* 10 steps balancing a glass of water**. Then she went the **fastest 100 meters (328 feet) with a can balanced on head** in 2 minutes and 55 seconds.

Abbie Girl, a Kelpie,
loves going to the beach
to show off her talent.
In 2011, she surfed a wave
for more than 351 feet!
That's the **longest
open-water wave
surfed by a dog**!

Two dogs have jumped
to great lengths!
Taz, shown here,
and Chochiti are tied
for the record for the **farthest
jump by a dog
in a dock-jumping competition**.
Both pooches leaped 31 feet!

A Lab retriever–border collie cross,
Rose set the record for
the **most discs caught and held
in the mouth at one time**.
Rose caught and held 7 discs.

Davy Whippet holds the record
for the **longest flying disc throw
caught by a dog**.
He caught a disc that was thrown
from 402 feet away!

Labradoodle Ranmaru

can get anything

if he flutters his eyelashes.

At 5.9 inches long

he boasts the **longest**

doggy eyelash.

Milly, a Chihuahua,

is the **smallest living dog**.

She is only 3.8 inches tall.

Puggy, a Pekingese,
has the **longest**
tongue in the dog world,
at 4.5 inches long.
He has the record licked!